2ND EDITION

PERFORMANCE

LEVEL 3B

PIANO
Adventures® *by Nancy and Randall Faber*
THE BASIC PIANO METHOD

CONTENTS

FABER
PIANO ADVENTURES®
3042 Creek Drive
Ann Arbor, Michigan 48108

The Medieval Piper

Key of ____ Major / Minor (circle)

N. Faber

Moderato (♩ = 108-132)

5/18

f-p on repeat

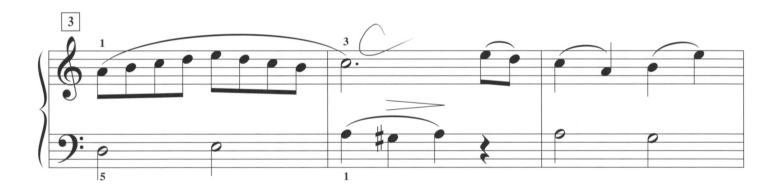

Repeat p

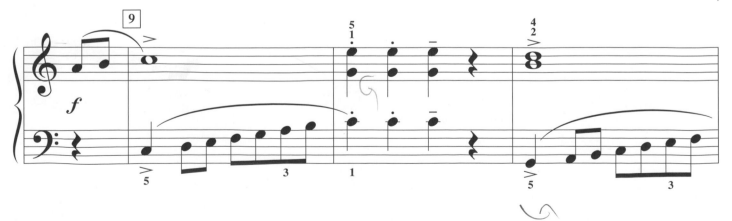

f

📖 Lesson pp.10–11 (Fiesta España)

FF118

Your teacher may demonstrate the optional trill (*tr*).

Extend the trill for the final measure.

This graceful waltz uses four minor chords to give a
mysterious effect.

L.H. Warm-up

• Play several times until it's easy!
  Can you play with your eyes closed?

Mysterious Ballet

Key of E Minor

N. Faber

Gracefully (= 88-100)

German Dance

Key of ___ Major/Minor

Ludwig van Beethoven
(1770-1827, Germany)
original form

Moderato (♩ = 100-116)

f-*p* on repeat

DISCOVERY

Name the opening **interval** for each section.

Lesson pp.18–19 (Rage Over a Lost Penny)

Repeated Notes
Quick, repeated notes are often played using changing fingers. This helps keep the hand relaxed.

R.H. Warm-up
• Play at slow, moderate, and faster tempos.

Tum-Balalaika*

Key of ____ Major / Minor

Jewish Folk Song
arranged

Moderately (♩ = 126-144)

*The *balalaika* is a 3-string Russian folk instrument with a triangular body. It is similar to the guitar or mandolin.

DISCOVERY Name the harmony for the last measure of each line (**i** or **V7**).

Whispers of the Wind

Key of ____ Major/Minor

R. Faber

Slowly, expressively (♩=88-96)

Lesson pp.27–29 (Legend of Madrid)

FF118

- First practice hands separately.
- Then practice hands together at an *adagio* (very slow) tempo, and then an *andante* (walking speed) tempo.

Minuet in G

(from the Notebook for Anna Magdalena Bach)

Christian Petzold
(1677-1733, Germany)
original form

(light thumb)

(light thumb)

Lesson pp.34–35 (Humoresque)

FF118

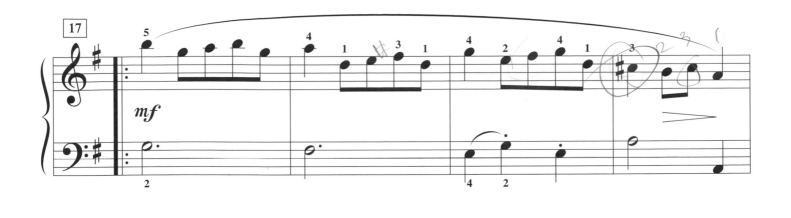

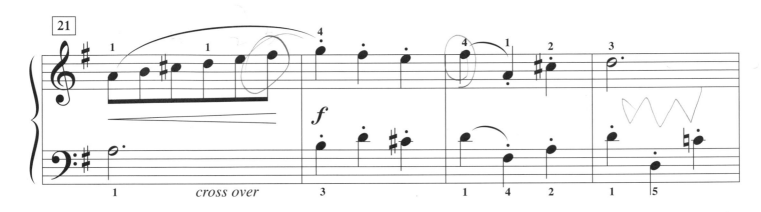

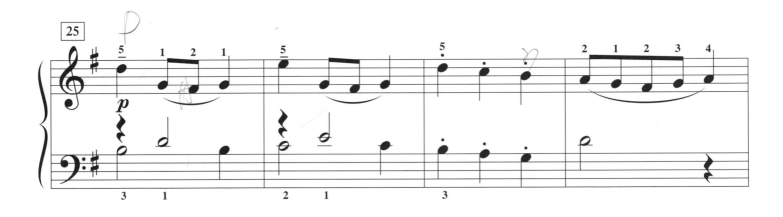

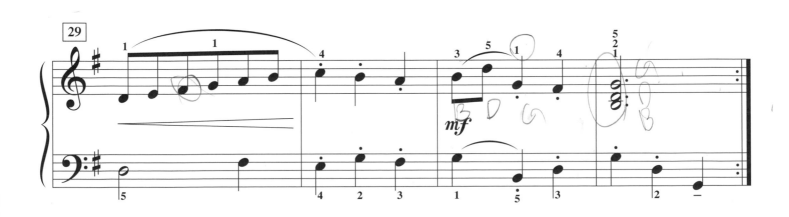

DISCOVERY

Can you find the **leading tone** in *measure 31?* Does it resolve up to the **tonic**?

13

Hava Nagila

Key of _____ Major/Minor

Hava nagila means "Let us rejoice and be happy."

Hebrew Folk Song

*Omit the top note of the L.H. octaves for smaller hands.

14 📖 Lesson pp.36–37 (The Bear)

FF1182

DISCOVERY Find a 2-measure **pattern** and **sequence** on the first page.

Find a 4-measure **pattern** and **sequence** on the second page.

- This piece uses a broken chord accompaniment. Name the **harmony** in the boxes.

All Through the Night

Key of ____ Major/Minor

Gently (♩=84-92)

Traditional Welsh Air
arranged

Ex. D

DISCOVERY Circle the correct form of this piece.

A B A   A A B A coda   A A B B   A B coda

100 Degree Blues

Key of ____ Major/Minor

N. Faber

📖Lesson pp.46–47 (The Piano Playin' Chocolate Eater's Blues)

FF1181

DISCOVERY This piece follows a 12-bar blues chord progression. Where does the harmony change to the **IV chord**? *measure* _____ The **V chord**? *measure* _____

*Omit the top note of the R.H. octaves for smaller hands.

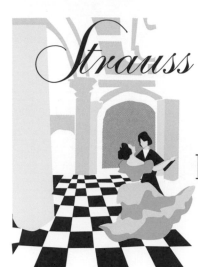

Strauss

Blue Danube Waltz

Key of ____ Major/Minor

Johann Strauss, Jr.
(1825-1899, Austria)
arranged

Moderate waltz tempo (♩ = 100-132)

DISCOVERY

Point out two lines of music that use only notes from the **C major chord**.

Fascination

Key of ____ Major/Minor

Fermo Dante Marchetti
(1876-1940, Italy)
arranged

Moderately slow (♩ = 88-120)

📖 Lesson pp.52–53 (Swing Low, Sweet Chariot)

FF1182

DISCOVERY

Point out four **D major** arpeggios and two **E minor** arpeggios.

Hint: First play hands separately, observing the staccatos, slurs, and dynamics.

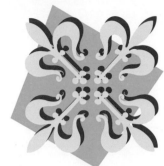

Bagatelle* in G

Allegro moderato (♩ = 72-88)

N. Faber

*A bagatelle is a short musical piece, usually written for the piano.

Circle the form of this piece: **A B**   **A B A coda**   **A B A**   **A B C**

*Omit the bottom note of the L.H. octave for smaller hands.

On Wings of Song

Secondo

Felix Mendelssohn
(1809-1847, Germany)
arranged

Memorize measures 12-13 for page turn.

FF1182

On Wings of Song

Primo

Felix Mendelssohn
(1809-1847, Germany)
arranged

📖 Lesson pp.58–59 (Gypsy Camp)   27

"Star-Spangled Rhythm"

The dotted eighth to 16th

$$ \text{♪.} \quad \text{♪} = \text{♩} $$
1 e + a   1 e + a

- Listen to your teacher play the opening three notes of *The Star-Spangled Banner*. Then imitate the rhythm.

- Circle each ♫ in this piece.
  (This rhythm is explored further in Level 4.)

The Star-Spangled Banner

Words by Francis Scott Key
Music by John Stafford Smith
arranged

Proudly (♩ = 66-76)

Oh,___ say can you see, by the dawn's ear - ly light, What so proud - ly we hailed at the twi - light's last gleam - ing. Whose broad

*For smaller hands, omit the bottom note of the L.H. octaves and adjust fingering.

DISCOVERY Point out the following in this piece to your teacher:

an accidental	parallel 6ths for the R.H.
C major one-octave arpeggio	a grace note
G major one-octave arpeggio	C major chord inversions